Greater Than a Tourist Myrtle Beach South Carolina USA

50 Travel Tips from a Local

Amy A. Sylvestre

Order Information: To order this title please email lbrenenc@gmail.com or visit GreaterThanATourist.com. A bulk discount can be provided.

Cover Template Creator: Lisa Rusczyk Ed. D. using Canva.
Cover Creator: Lisa Rusczyk Ed. D.
Image: https://pixabay.com/en/ocean-south-carolina-coast-travel-465401/

Lock Haven, PA
All rights reserved.
ISBN: 9781549837166

>TOURIST

BOOK DESCRIPTION

Are you excited about planning your next trip?

Do you want to try something new?

Would you like some guidance from a local?

If you answered yes to any of these questions, then this Greater Than a Tourist book is for you.

Greater than a Tourist- Myrtle Beach, South Carolina, USA by Amy Sylvestre offers the inside scoop on Myrtle Beach. Most travel books tell you how to sightsee. Although there's nothing wrong with that, as a part of the Greater than a Tourist series, this book will give you tips from someone who lives at your next travel destination. In these pages, you'll discover local advice that will help you throughout your trip. Travel like a local. Slow down and get to know the people and the culture of a place. By the time you finish this book, you will be eager and prepared to travel to your next destination.

Amy A. Sylvestre

TABLE OF CONTENTS

13. Go South Of Myrtle Beach To Pawley's Island

14. Cruise The Strip

15. Zip Through The Trees

17. Go Family Fun Camping

18. Have Dinner In Murrell's Inlet

19. Save Money At Tanger Outlets

20. Enjoy Fresh Seafood

21. Fall In Love In Brookgreen Gardens

22. Stay Up Late

23. Lunch At Dagwood's

24. Have A Glass Of Wine

25. Scream For Ice Cream

26. Avoid Biker Weeks

27. Take The Kids

28. Date Night At Collector's

29. After The Beach Walk At Market Commons

30. Go Crabbing At Night

31. Take A Stroll On The Boardwalk

32. Adventure By Helicopter

33. Don't Over Do It At The Buffet

34. Go Barefoot

35. Connect Spiritually

36. Fill Up On Pancakes

37. Take A Friend On The BrewCrew

38. Enjoy The Show

39. Go Boating

41. Take A Cruise on the Intracoastal Waterway

42. Hit A Few Rounds Of Golf

43. Pretend You are NASCAR Legend, Dale Earnhardt

44. Go On Safari With The Kids

45. Don't Skip Breakfast

46. Shop At Broadway At The Beach

47. Go Shagging

48. Get Splashed At Water Parks

49. Fill Up On Down Home Cooking

50. Take Care Of You

Our Story

Notes

DEDICATION

This book is dedicated to my parents, Joe and Cathy Alexander. My childhood is full of wonderful memories that include bumper boats, cotton candy, corn dogs, boardwalks, ice cream and the sandy beach because of summer trips to Myrtle Beach, South Carolina. Now my children will know all the local spots as they experience them first hand on family trips with their amazing grandparents.

Amy A. Sylvestre

ABOUT THE AUTHOR

Amy Sylvestre is a wife, mom, and writer from North Carolina. Amy fell in love with her husband walking through the streets of New York. Amy enjoys time with her family, a good book, the beach with family, and quoting the show, "*Friends*." After completing her Master's Degree focused on International Relations, she has ended up living in several major cities in the United States. She has traveled around much of Europe and India. She also spent two summers in South Africa and six months in France. Amy vacationed during the summer in Myrtle Beach throughout her childhood. The year after she was married, she called Myrtle Beach home.

Amy A. Sylvestre

HOW TO USE THIS BOOK

The Greater Than a Tourist book series was written by someone who has lived in an area for over three months. The goal of this book is to help travelers either dream or experience different locations by providing opinions from a local. The author has made suggestions based on their own experiences. Please do your own research before traveling to the area in case the suggested places are unavailable.

Amy A. Sylvestre

FROM THE PUBLISHER

Traveling can be one of the most important parts of a person's life. The anticipation and memories that you have are some of the best. As a publisher of the Greater Than a Tourist book series, as well as the popular 50 Things to Know book series, we strive to help you learn about new places, spark your imagination, and inspire you. Wherever you are and whatever you do I wish you safe, fun, and inspiring travel.

Lisa Rusczyk Ed. D.

CZYK Publishing

Amy A. Sylvestre

WELCOME TO > TOURIST

Amy A. Sylvestre

INTRODUCTION

Myrtle Beach has so many different personalities that appeal to families, singles, retired seniors, and children. Whether coming for a summer vacation with the whole family, on a honeymoon, or with a group of singles, there is much to discover in this famous beach town. Be sure to take in the sights by walking the Strip of the Grand Strand with a corndog and a milk shake. There are arcades, adventures, carnival rides and of course, the beach! You won't miss the souvenir shops located around town where you can find little trinkets, t-shirts, hats, beach towels, sun screen, beach chairs, and other Myrtle Beach memorabilia. There is great seafood, beautiful sights, amazing restaurants, and a relaxed atmosphere. Many visitors will say that there is something magical about taking a leisurely walk on the beach early in the morning and then stopping at a local eatery for a delicious breakfast before starting a busy day of golf or seeing the sights. Whether you prefer, the shows, adventure rides, restaurants, visiting local shops, or the water parks, you will leave with a memorable vacation! You can choose to enjoy soaking up the sun or being active on a bike ride. There is so much variety in Myrtle Beach but if you are like me then the beach is your main reason for going here and you will agree with this little saying, *"Life takes you down many paths but my favorite ones lead to the beach."* There is certainly something for just about everyone from every walk of life in this iconic vacation spot. After just a few days, you will fall in love with this historic, fun beach town and start to plan your next trip! Bonnes vacances!

Amy A. Sylvestre

1. Head To The Beach

Myrtle Beach is a place to have adventure, soak in the sun, get away from stress, and relax. Pack up the kids, bring some snacks and a beach chair! The best place to really experience all that Myrtle Beach has to offer is on the beach. You can enjoy the water, playing in the sand, walking on the piers, laying out, and strolling up and down the beach. It is also fun to people-watch and guess where everyone is from. People come from all over the world come here just to get a taste of what Myrtle Beach has offer. So, put on your sunscreen, grab your umbrella, and bring your boogie board. Spend the day just enjoying and relaxing as you swim in the salt water and listen to the waves crashing on the sand.

2. Be Smart

No matter where you travel, it is important to be wise with where you go, what time you go and with whom you travel. Myrtle Beach is no different so you should take care of yourself and be alert. There is much beauty to enjoy and fun to be had in this vacation town. Myrtle Beach is a popular travel town for recent graduates and without fail, every single year, young people who go out alone in the middle of the night tragically end up missing. So, go out with people you know well. Don't walk the streets alone. Don't walk the beach alone. Don't take drinks from someone you don't know. Don't leave valuables in plain sight on your beach towel or in your cars. Don't give out your personal information to strangers. Always be aware that tourists are

targeted for theft. Have a blast in this awesome little beach town but be smart!

3. Explore the MarshWalk

There are so many activities and adventures in Myrtle Beach but if you are ready to enjoy the sights of the low country, go and take a walk on the wooden boardwalk in Murrell's Inlet, all the while experiencing this quaint little fishing village. You will likely see creatures like the great white herons, blue herons, and even possibly pelicans. This area boast delicious seafood, live music, great views and a relaxed atmosphere. Even if you aren't going to the area for a meal, you can stroll along this waterfront boardwalk. It is beautiful during the day but my favorite time to go is at sunset. You can enjoy watching the fishing boats returning after a long day at sea. If you are looking for a bit of excitement, then know that live music and other local events often take place along the MarshWalk. If you are looking for a great place to relax after a day of adventures, check out this area breathtaking place and the view is free of charge!

4. Have A Meal In Little River

Little River is a laid back little area north of the Grand Strand of Myrtle Beach. Locals love this area for its unique personality and hometown feel. Save your appetite and head to Little River. You will find some amazing places for breakfast, lunch, dinner, snacks, and desserts. You definitely shouldn't leave hungry. Locals prefer The Little River Deli for their breakfast sandwiches. You can enjoy soups, salads, and sandwiches at Jilla's Gourmet Kitchen. If you are looking for pub food and to watch the game, stop at Drinking Class Sports bar. You can also jump in with the locals and show off your karaoke skills. If you are looking for a delicious breakfast buffet, check out Mama Jean's Restaurant. For a drink at the bar and some live music, choose Swing Bridge Saloon. Have a glass of wine and some delicious crème brulee at Brentwood Wine Bistro. If you are looking for a bit of adventure, go on a dolphin tour with Voyager Deep Sea Fishing & Dolphin Cruises. There is much to enjoy just north of Myrtle Beach in Little River.

5. See All Of Myrtle Beach On The SkyWheel

The SkyWheel is the the second-tallest Ferris wheel in North America and is located right on the Grand Strand Strip in Myrtle Beach. You won't miss if you take a drive on Ocean Boulevard. If you don't have a fear of heights, this is a wonderful experience to see over the ocean and the lights of this little tourist town. Bring your camera and take some awesome photos of the ocean right from the ride. It is a fun attraction during the day but also at night. Grab some friends and take in the views! Have fun!

6. Stock Up On Groceries

If you are staying somewhere with a kitchen and plan on making some meals, you won't have any problem finding places for your standard needs at stores like Walmart and Food Lion. But, if you are looking for fresh seafood then make a stop at Seas Seafood Shop. You can also get fresh produce and artisanal Italian products at Lee's Farmer's Market. Don't miss out on their deli as well as their many homemade goods including homemade pastas and cheeses. Yum!

7. Pretend You Are Under The Ocean

Many tourist towns have cool spots you don't want to miss but none quite like Ripley's Aquarium located at Broadway at the Beach . This spot is a must see if you have children. You could spend most of your day just wondering around and seeing the exhibits of all kinds of sea creatures. There are parts of the Aquarium where you will feel like you are under the water with the sharks. You can see the staff go into these massive tanks and feed the fish. You can also go to the shallow water area and pet a stingray. I've heard a rumor that for a price, and at certain times, you can spend the night in this amazing place. If you are traveling on a budget with children, you will want to plan ahead for this excursion. Be on the lookout for the coupon books found outside of many restaurants and hotels. Ripley's Aquarium often has discounts listed here. Your kids will talk about this adventure long after your beach vacation has ended.

8. Go For The Burger

Of course you came to the ocean to enjoy some delicious and fresh seafood but there are some well-loved burger joints that you don't want to miss. Hamburger Joe's is a local favorite and the walls are decorated in an interesting way. It is covered with dollar bills (and no you can't have any of them.)! They are reasonably priced and offer delicious comfort food in a laidback, beach town atmosphere. River City Café has several locations and is also a beloved spot of delicious variety of burgers. My favorite location is in Surfside Beach.

9. Stay Healthy At Bay Naturals

It is true you are on vacation and want to have some treats along the way but when you are ready for a light, healthy, delicious meal, plan a meal or grocery trip to Bay Naturals. This little local secret is a wonderful restaurant and store for people who want to eat really healthy while enjoying every bite. There are many delicious meal options as well as your choice of smoothies and fresh pressed juices. Be sure that their homemade, clean desserts will hit the spot and keep your diet light! There are two Bay Naturals locations in the Myrtle Beach area. Enjoy!

10. Kayak at Huntington State Park

The locals love the beach just as much as the tourists who come from all over the world, but they typically like to take their beach activities a little off the beaten path. At Huntington State Park, you will find a wide and pristine Grand Strand beach with picnic tables and fewer crowds than what you find off the infamous Ocean Boulevard. If you want a place to bring your dog and a laidback day of bird watching, camping, and fishing, this is perfect spot to spend the day. If you love being part of nature you will be excited to see loggerhead turtles as well as other endangered plant and animal species up close and personal. If you are lucky, you might even spot an alligator. Stay clear! A great landmark called the Atalaya is located here and is a Moorish-style home of the Huntingtons, who were philanthropists who left the park as their legacy. Thousands of art lovers attend the prestigious Atalaya Arts and Crafts Festival held each year in September. There is a small fee to enter the park so check online for pricing.

"The ocean stirs the heart, inspires the imagination

and brings eternal joy to the soul."

Wyland

Amy A. Sylvestre

11. You Can't Miss Putt Putt

No matter what part of Myrtle Beach you decide to stay in, there will be many choices for a fun round of mini-golf. If you are looking for activity away from the water, this is just the right pick! Many of the Putt Putt courses are designed with certain themes like pirates, tropical, and shipwrecks. Your kiddos will have a blast checking out all of the different designs as they challenge themselves to make a hole in one! A few places to practice your mini-golfing skills are Shipwreck Island Adventure, Black Pearl Mini Golf, and Aloha Mini Golf.

12. Fish Off The Garden City Pier

Garden City is a small beach town slightly south of Myrtle Beach. This area is a bit of a quieter and slower paced than what you will find in the center of the lights and sounds on the Grand Strand Strip. Enjoy some lunch at the café, bring your pole for some fishing, let the kids enjoy the arcade, or simply take a leisurely walk and take in the scene of the vast Atlantic ocean. There is no fee to enjoy these memorable views. There are also many local fishermen who frequent the pier for sport, fun, and to catch their own dinner. If it is a rainy day, head to the end of the pier for a bit of covering.

13. Go South Of Myrtle Beach To Pawley's Island

Pawleys Island is a picturesque seaside town located thirty minutes south of the Strip and is on the very south end of the Grand Strand of Myrtle Beach. This area has so much to offer. Pawley's Island just might be what you need if you are looking for an area a bit more tranquil and a place to experience the beauty of the Lowcountry landscape. You can also enjoy the famous, old, classic homes called Cypress cottages. There are large areas of undeveloped marshland as well as beautiful rivers. This beach town community is not that far south of Myrtle Beach and offers many higher end opportunities including places to stay and restaurants. If you are looking for a finer experience, you might just want to stay a bit south of Myrtle. A few restaurants locals love are Bistro 217, Rustic Table and Captain Dave's Dockside. If you'd like to enjoy the gorgeous weather and dine outside, head to Frank's Outback or Bistro 419. Pretty all the locals will agree that Perrone's is the absolute best. Whether looking for low country cuisine, a finer meal or an outdoors-enthusiasts, you will appreciate all that is offered by a vacation in Pawleys Island.

14. Cruise The Strip

For generations students have made their way to Myrtle Beach to enjoy the sun, ocean, and fun offered here. As quoted in the movie, *Shag*, students plan their trips here saying, *"I'm going to Myrtle Beach to meet boys. What are you doing?"* The Strip is a classic sight right out of a movie scene. People covered in sunscreen, music blasting, windows down, hollering, "hey y'all!" to the passersby. You don't take Ocean Boulevard on The Strip for a shortcut ride to get somewhere on time. The traffic is slow, the scenes are free, and the experience memorable. You pick this route because it is leisurely, fun, exciting, and unexpected. If you haven't seen the movie, *"Shag,"* watch it before your trip to get an idea of the vibes you will experience in this iconic little beach town with lots of personality.

15. Zip Through The Trees

Of course you want to soak up the sun on the ocean as much as possible but if you'd like to take a break from building sand castles, plan a few hours to check out, Go Ape Treetop Adventure. You can zipline through the trees for up to three hours. If you are brave then you can try the Tarzan swings or tackle the amazing obstacles up in trees as high as fifty feet. This adventure is great families of all ages as well youth groups or other folks looking for a memorable adventure. Check them out and ask for group rates. Have fun zipping!

16. Stay Here

There are many ocean front resorts and hotels on Ocean Boulevard. Depending on your desires, Embassy Suites in North Myrtle Beach might be what you are looking for. While this hotel is a bit dated, it is reasonably priced, comfortable enough, and ocean front. They also are reasonably priced which also helps! Dunes Village Resort is a great place to stay and a ton of fun for the kids. They have lots to do indoor and outside. It has also recently been renovated with nice sizes rooms that include a modest kitchen, a washer and dryer, and great linens. The Marriott Grande Dunes is well loved and offers great pools, ideal customer service, and convenient restaurants on site. This hotel has also recently been renovated. I hope this helps you narrow down the many choices for lodging in Myrtle Beach.

17. Go Family Fun Camping

Perhaps you didn't know that camping was a way of life for folks who visit this amazing little beach town but there is an amazing option for you and your family and friends. If you think you know what it means to go camping then you've not been to Lakewood Camping Resort where their slogan is *"More Than Just Camping."* This oceanfront site is over 200 acres and offers campsites, villas, RV parks as well as personally owned properties. Each of these areas has access directly to half a mile of sandy beach. There are amenities included in your stay like the fantastic family friendly water park and splash area. In the area you will also find convenient places for shopping, dining, and entertainment. This camp ground also offers special events from time to time. If you are looking for a cost effective trip with groups of any size, the Lakewood facilities can cater to any sized group. The staff is accommodating and there are rooms that can used for different gatherings at the Information Center. The Coffee House is a great place for more personal gatherings. Your kids will thank you for bringing them to Lakewood Camping Resort!

18. Have Dinner In Murrell's Inlet

Murrell's Inlet is a short drive just south of the strip in Myrtle Beach. If you are looking for a laidback atmosphere with beautiful views of the marshland, this is the place to linger over a wonderful dinner. You will have the choice of many locally loved restaurants. Russell's is known for the fresh seafood they purchase at the docks every morning. Dead Dog Salon, Perrone's and River City Café are also spots that locals regularly enjoy. You will enjoy many different options of low country cuisine that include delicious steaks and fresh seafood. Some of these restaurant boast award-winning chefs and live music. You will likely want to visit this area several times on your trip because the vibe is so different from the more hype areas on the main Strip of the Grand Strand of Myrtle Beach. Enjoy all that Murrells Inlet has to offer you and your family!

19. Save Money At Tanger Outlets

If you are like me and like to find a deal, I will suggest spending some time at the Tanger Outlets located just before you reach Myrtle Beach. There are actually two different locations to in the area. Even if it is summer, this is a great place to get early gifts for Christmas. Your dollar will go much further here. You will find deals on designer labels at places like Kate Spade, Coach, and Michael Kors. If you need some new athletic gear, you will feel like you hit the jackpot with if you can stop at Reebok, New Balance, and Lululemon. If you want to get the kids ready for back to school, you will be thrilled to know that these outlets include stores like Carter's Babies and Kids, Gymboree, and The Children's Place. You also enjoy a great meal at places like Steak N Shake, Five Guys, and Stillhouse Barbecue. For dessert you can have a treat at Auntie Anne's Pretzel Perfect or Ben Jerry's Ice Cream but my favorite is enjoying a special local treat at The Fudgery. This is a great place to go if there is rain.

20. Enjoy Fresh Seafood

If you love seafood and prefer it to be caught the morning you plan to eat it, then you Myrtle Beach is a perfect place for you. You will have so many options for delicious, fresh seafood. For a great price and delicious choices, check out a local favorite called Mr. fish! Locals say that Inlet Crab House is excellent and consistent. You will know this because the place will be full of local folks who coming regularly. Plan ahead because you will have to go early to even get a table at Bimini's Seafood and Oyster Bar but the food is awesome and worth the effort. Other locals prefer Giant Crab for their fresh seafood. Calabash is a great place to enjoy picks of the day and you won't regret choosing Dockside Seafood House. If you head to North Myrtle you will enjoy the atmosphere, personable staff, and great food at Goodfellas Seafood. Needless to say, there is so many delicious options for fresh caught seafood in Myrtle Beach! I'm sure you will find a favorite that your family will frequent on all your future trips to Myrtle Beach!

Amy A. Sylvestre

"Who else has held the oceans in his hand? Who has measured off the heavens with his fingers? Who else knows the weight of the earth or has weighed the mountains and hills on a scale?"

Amy A. Sylvestre

21. Fall In Love In Brookgreen Gardens

If you are looking for a sweet surprise, look no further than Brookgreen Gardens! You will be shocked to know what is hiding just inside the entrance of this gorgeous little secret garden. Most tourists miss out on this amazing local treasure. The beauty of this place is amazing and worth your time. You can enjoy a romantic boat ride and then visit the butterfly house. You can experience the beauty of art, sculptures, and history as you take in the grounds. You can also explore the zoo and the breathtaking gardens. Take a moment and look at some pictures online and you will see why the locals love to spend afternoons on these amazing grounds. Make a stop at the little shop. If you are going to be in the area for a while, you can sign up for classes offered here as well. There is fee for admission which is valid for a full week. You can receive a discount if your ticket is purchased online.

22. Stay Up Late

After a long day in the sun and bit of a nap, go out with friends and hear some amazing live music, and don't forget your dancing shoes! Go check out the Spanish Gallion for some beach music, drinks, and dancing. Some other late night places to visit are Eighty Eight's Piano Bar, Ocean Annie's Beach Bar, and Malibu's Beach Bar. Just a little south of Myrtle, you will find some great places to sit outdoors and enjoy the beautiful weather and local bands. A few local favorites are The Wicked Tuna, Dead Dog Saloon, Bovine's, and Dave's Dockside. Enjoy the music, the locals, the dancing, the view, and the drinks!

23. Lunch At Dagwood's

There are plenty of places to grab a sandwich in Myrtle Beach and you would probably not even notice this local shop but don't miss out. Dagwood's Deli is a beloved lunch spot for many locals and even regular vacationers are sure to stop by for their favorite sandwich. I don't know if it is the fresh bread or the mayonnaise but I love "The Southern" which is a turkey sandwich with a twist from Dagwood's. Their portions are generous and don't forget to get a pickle too! They have parking but you can also walk from the beach.

24. Have A Glass Of Wine

If you are ready to relax with a nice drink, plan to make a stop at Duplin Winery. There is a new location at Barefoot Landing in North Myrtle Beach. They are known for their consistency and quality as they strive to produce wines that capture the spirit of their heritage. After exploring and shopping in Barefoot, end the day with a nice glass of wine that the locals love. Enjoy!

25. Scream For Ice Cream

Nothing beats a great ice cream cone or milk shake after a hot day at the beach. It has become a tradition with my family to go to Painter's Ice Cream in Garden City. They have several locations including one on the Garden City Pier. You can get their Vanna Banana named for Wheel of Fortune's, Vanna White, who is a local. If you want a 'no kids' ice cream parlor loved by the locals, then head to North Myrtle Beach to Sea Blue for a delicious treat. Many locals also love Calabash Creamery for their homemade treats with gourmet flavors. Some of their unique treats are the peanut butter and jelly, candy galore, and Carolina sunshine. Tourists who come to Myrtle regularly include on this ice cream shop on their "must stop" list during their vacations. There are some great shops to visit in this area as well to take the time to walk around as you finish your treat. Some other well-loved local ice cream shops are Calahan's and Kirk's Ice Cream. If you love a coke or root beer float, you must go to Johnny Rockets at Broadway at the Beach!

26. Avoid Biker Weeks

There are only few reasons to go to Myrtle Beach during Biker Weeks. If you own leather chaps, like sitting in bumper to bumper traffic for hours, and enjoying riding motorcycles with very little clothing, then you may not want to heed to my advice. Otherwise, biker week will make a saint lose his or her religion. Traffic literally does not move. Bikers from all walks of life take over the main roads and enjoy just sitting around showing off what the *Good Lord* gave them (meaning they are wearing very little clothing). Besides the massive inconvenience this could bring to your supposed vacation, this week also is not known as the safest time to be in Myrtle Beach. If you want to know more, just look online (without your kids) for images of Biker Week and to get more details. Now you can't say I didn't warn you. Just pick another weekend to go to Myrtle Beach to avoid all the craziness that comes with Biker Week!

27. Take The Kids

There are so many places that your kids are going to love in Myrtle Beach. If you are looking for a place that is "toddler friendly," then look no further than *Savannah's Playground* located in the Market Commons area. It is seriously amazing for your whole family. They have zip lines geared towards toddler-aged children. They also have sensory activities, tons of swings, and a musical exploration area that your kids are going to love. There is also a water play area that is just perfect for your little ones. You can also take a walk around the Market Commons Complex and feed the ducks and geese around the water.

28. Date Night At Collector's

So after you have spent the whole day chasing the little ones around on the beach, take the time for date night with your special someone. If you are looking for a unique, local place to unwind and enjoy the finer things that Myrtle Beach has to offer, get out of your beach bum clothes, and plan a dinner date at Collectors Café and Gallery. You can enjoy a delicious, romantic meal and also take in some local art at the same time. They serve dinner from 5:30 to 10:30 in the evening and they also take reservations. Whether you pick the filet mignon, rack of lamb, spiced salmon, or the seared duck breast, you are in for a delightful meal. Pair your meal with their signature cocktails and then top it all off with tiramisu, coconut cake, or my favorite, the crème brulee. You won't regret this lovely night out at a local favorite.

29. After The Beach Walk At Market Commons

Market Commons has a little bit of everything for everyone on your trip. Many locals actually live in this area and enjoy all this true urban village community has to offer. There are many local retail shops to find a special souvenir. This area offers entertainment, shopping, dining, and a great place for a walk after dinner or an afternoon run. I have so many favorite restaurants in this area. I will suggest a local favorite, Tupelo Honey Café. The food is fresh, Southern food that they claim is good for you soul. I won't blame you can you go here for brunch and dinner! The kids will love to feed the ducks and geese while walking around the water in this area. At the entrance to Market Commons you will find Warbird Park. There are several old fighter aircraft that are "Dedicated to The Men And Women Of The United States Air Force." There is no charge to stop and take in a bit of history and grab a picture with these amazing fighter jets. There are also some shaded picnic tables where you can stop and have a meal.

Amy A. Sylvestre

30. Go Crabbing At Night

One of my favorite times in Myrtle Beach is after the sun goes
down and it is not for all of the night life the town offers. Pack a
flash light and when it is completely dark, take some friends and
go for a long walk on the beach. Even if you don't want to actually
catch the crabs, it is quite fun to shine your light down the beach
and watch them scurrying away. You will need to find an area that
is not full of people and away from lots of light. Be sure to watch
out for jellyfish that may have washed ashore. It will feel so nice to
be out on the beach at night with less crowds. Enjoy a less touristy
time of day on the beach!

"In every outthrust headland, in every curving beach,

in every grain of sand there is the story of the earth."

Rachel Carson

Amy A. Sylvestre

31. Take A Stroll On The Boardwalk

No matter your age, going for a walk on the boardwalk is something you must do during your visit to Myrtle Beach. It is a tradition that has happened for many generations and you don't want to miss out! When the original Pavilion was open here, there were rides and an older style Ferris Wheel much smaller than the SkyWheel. Being here brings back memories for me and is a great place to build new ones. There is something so special about walking around this area and seeing all the carnival type rides, playing some arcade games, and enjoying a corndog, funnel cake and ice cream. I love this area in particular at dusk when you can feel the breeze of the ocean, the heat of the sun, and the pulse of the people. Take some friends, find a photo booth, and make some memories. Have a blast and be safe!

32. Adventure By Helicopter

Perhaps you are like me and enjoy watching the hit TV shows, The Bachelor and The Bachelorette. If so, you've probably observed that there is never a season without at least one helicopter ride. So, go to Helicopter Adventures near Broadway at the Beach, and pretend you are on your very own reality TV show and jump in for a unique adventure. You will be surprised at how affordable it is to see the whole of this beach town from the sky. Don't try to film it or take pictures the whole time or you will miss out on just enjoying it. Based on your budget, there are shorter rides that stay right in the area and longer rides that will take you further north. Most all the rides will take you over the ocean and if you are lucky, you just might spot a shark or a sea turtle. Be sure to tell them my pilot husband, Corey, sent you. He worked there several years ago.

33. Don't Over Do It At The Buffet

We have a joke in our family about buffets because of the restaurant, Captain Crab Calabash Seafood. If we have thoroughly indulged and feel overly full, we will say, "I calabashed that meal!" It is so easy to want to try everything that this amazing buffet has to offer and leave feeling super full! There are more than hundred items on the buffet at a time. There are a lot of buffets in town but this is our favorite! Enjoy the all-you-can-eat crab leg with a cup of melted butter. For another great buffet option in the area check out, Captain Benjamin's Restaurant buffet that includes crab legs and steaks. They always include fried, steamed and baked seafood. They also have raw bar, salad bar, and you can finish your meal off at their amazing dessert bar.

34. Go Barefoot

Whether you enjoy seeing the local shops, the entertainment, or the restaurants, Barefoot Landing is a fun place to spend the day. You can simply walk around and enjoy the sights and shops or you can sit down for a nice meal. Barefoot Landing is located in the northern part of the Grand Strand and a perfect place to enjoy your vacation. Many locals enjoy the wine at Duplin winery but the biggest adventure just might be at Preservation Station where there is a living tiger exhibit. You can get up close and personal with only glass between you and the 500 pound adult tigers. You can also have the opportunity to interact with tiger cubs and apes! Don't miss one of the most unique adventures offered in Myrtle Beach!

35. Connect Spiritually

Instead of sleeping in on Sunday morning, don't miss out on an amazing community of people at Surfside Presbyterian Church. The whole congregation is warm, welcoming, and genuine. They will likely have snacks and coffee out before and after the service. If you tell them that you heard about them from someone from the nonprofit ministry, Campus Outreach, you will likely get an offer to enjoy a homecooked meal. Great folks here! Tell Pastor Riddle I said hello!

36. Fill Up On Pancakes

There are so many places to enjoy breakfast in Myrtle Beach but one of my favorites for a pancake breakfast is Dino's House of Pancakes in North Myrtle Beach. This restaurant is a classic, down-to-earth mainstay for locals and visitors. They serve a traditional American breakfast as well as lunch favorites, in a low-key atmosphere. They have lots of other delicious breakfast dishes in addition to their famous pancakes. Load up on carbs before your day at the beach! They are only open until 2pm so plan to go before your day at the beach or take a break and head over for lunch!

37. Take A Friend On The BrewCrew

The BrewCrew is a local favorite! If you'd like to enjoy a drink and take a cruise on the beautiful marshlands then head to the East Coast BrewBoat. You can take someone for a romantic date or go with a group of friends for a great time on the water! You can also reserve the BrewBoat for special events and parties. Enjoy the music, drinks, conversation and of course, the views!

Amy A. Sylvestre

38. Enjoy The Show

There are so many different shows that you could see a new one each night you are in Myrtle Beach. You can see a bit of Gospel, Broadway, or a comedy show at the Alabama Theater. Catch Counting Crows or Hootie and The Blow Fish at the well-loved House of Blues. Enjoy dinner and a show with live animals at the Pirates' Voyage. No matter what you choose, the shows are well done, the food amazing, and the drinks cold. You'll be telling your friends about the shows just as much as the beach and sand itself.

39. Go Boating

Spend a day enjoying water adventures at Captain Dick's just south of Myrtle Beach in Murrells Inlet. Whether you prefer a pirate-ship adventure or parasailing, you've come to the right place. Plus, you can take the kids on a dolphin sightseeing cruises or a pontoon boat. If you want something a bit faster, you can rent a jet ski to crash against the waves of the Atlantic Ocean. For slower adventures, rent a kayak, peddle boat, or paddleboard. No matter what you choose, you are in for a good time on the water. This is a great place for families and you can stay for a delicious meal with live music after a day out on the water.

40. Let Them Eat Cake

You might be surprised that I am going to suggest that you visit Painter's Ice Cream for cake but I promise you won't be disappointed by your choice if you choose to eat the unbelievably amazing chocolate lovers cake. Don't get me wrong, their ice cream is also so tasty and this place is a complete local hangout. They have a new building as their original one was destroyed by a fire. It is a cute little ice parlor. My favorite is chocolate mixed with the coffee and I prefer it as a milkshake. Enjoy these delicious treats after a hot day in the southern sun!

"God's love is an ocean; you can see its beginning,

but not its end."

Rick Warren

Amy A. Sylvestre

41. Take A Cruise on the Intracoastal Waterway

Myrtle Beach has some special secrets and the Intracoastal Waterway is one of the best ones! The smooth water is a nice contrast to the crashing of the waves on the shore. The Barefoot Landing Marina is located in North Myrtle Beach. There you will find the Barefoot Princess Riverboat where you can enjoy several different cruises including sightseeing cruises, sunset cruises, dinner cruises. You will take in scenic beauty as you enjoy entertaining narration. They also offer dinner cruises where you will enjoy a delicious buffet while cruising. The buffet includes of Boneless BBQ Ribs, Grilled Chicken, Mashed Potatoes, Grilled Vegetables, and Tossed Salad. You will also have your choice of dessert and drinks. After you have dinner, you may relax on the top deck of the riverboat or dance on the second deck. One plus is that parking is free. Don't forget that the marina offers a pool, hot tub, exercise room, laundry, and a spa.

42. Hit A Few Rounds Of Golf

Golfers from all over the world know that Myrtle Beach is a place that should not be missed. Their 4.5-Star rated courses are creatively designed by some of the world's most renowned golf architects. Golfers will plan to come to Myrtle Beach year after year because of the many courses available. You won't just enjoy a round of golf that is suitable for all skill levels but also many of the courses are simply stunning! You get a spectacular view with your golf! Myrtle Beach golf will also allow you to take in the beautiful, lush vegetation as you relax and hit a few rounds.

43. Pretend You are NASCAR Legend, Dale Earnhardt

If you are looking for a fast paced adventure then make a pitstop at the NASCAR Racing Experience located at the Myrtle Beach Speedway next to Helicopter Adventures. This is a common place that tourists include in their vacations but the locals also approve. You will have a firsthand experience of racing NASCAR style. This attraction is perfect for the NASCAR race fan who has always dreamed of being behind the wheel of a real NASCAR race car just like some of the great drivers like Dale Earnhardt! You will need to sit through a brief instructional meeting with a Crew Chief and then you will be off to the races as you get a taste of what it is like to be a real NASCAR driver. Ready, set, GO!

44. Go On Safari With The Kids

When you started planning your trip to Myrtle Beach, you thought you might see some unique fish, crabs, or a jellyfish, and if you are really lucky, maybe a dolphin. But, did you ever consider seeing an elephant at the beach? Myrtle Beach Safari is a little piece of paradise where you can pretend you are in South Africa on a real safari. You can interact with some of the world's most unique animals. This is your chance to see eagles, feed elephants, and play with tiger cubs. You don't want to miss the apes! Plus, one of the world's largest cats called a liger, lives here for you to meet and enjoy! You, and your whole family, won't regret taking a little break from the water and sand to meet these amazing creatures. Go visit Myrtle Beach Safari and don't forget your camera! For more information about pricing and hours, check out their website.

45. Don't Skip Breakfast

Breakfast and brunch are two important meals in Myrtle Beach. Many hotels and resorts include delicious breakfast meals but on Sunday, don't miss out on the huge brunch selections at Chestnut Hill in North Myrtle brunch. If you are staying in Myrtle Beach, it will be worth the short drive north on Ocean Boulevard! You can also enjoy a memorable breakfast at Eggs Up Grill and Mammy's Kitchen. The food is so good, you won't need to eat again until it is time for dinner!

46. Shop At Broadway At The Beach

Broadway at the Beach is a place you must go while in Myrtle Beach. There are so many adventures, restaurants, entertaining events, and shops to see. You can pick neat souvenirs and gifts for those at home. You can see firsthand how the locals make fudge and taffy. They even will give you a sample. One of favorite places to go in Myrtle is a place where you step back in time with some live entertainment with your burger at Johnny's Rockets. Be sure to try Jimmy Buffet's Margaritaville and the Hard Rock Café shaped like a Pyramid. You can't miss that building! For seafood check out Original Shucker's Raw Bar, King Kong Sushi, or Landry's Seafood. For some down home southern cooking, enjoy a meal at Paula Deen's Family Kitchen or Sweet Carolina's. There are so many adventures to take in here. A few momentous activities are Broadway Grandprix, Old Tyme Portraits, and Wonderworks. Broadway at the Beach is also the place to be for the hottest night life in town. A few hot spots are Broadway

Louie's, Senor Frog's, and Wet Willie's.

47. Go Shagging

Shagging has a whole different meaning in Myrtle Beach, South Carolina than it does in London, England. Shagging is a dance that was born in the heart of Myrtle Beach. The 'Carolina Shag' is a swing dance done with a partner and primarily danced to Beach Music. It has had such an impact over the generations that since 1984 has been the Official State Dance of South Carolina. The name, Carolina Shag originated in Myrtle Beach in the 1930's. When you watch the locals dance the shag, you will see a mixture of some of the original basic steps being called the: Cuban Step, the Shuffle, and the Twinkle. To check out this local dance, be sure to go to Fat Harold's Beach Club and don't be scared to jump in and try it out for yourself. The locals would love to teach you and give you a whirl. You can do an online search and find videos of this local dance as well. It is smooth and beautiful! The best way to fully understand how shagging has affected the culture of this area is to watch the 1989 movie, "Shag." Now, get your dancing shoes and partner and head to Fat Harold's tonight!

48. Get Splashed At Water Parks

Water activities can be found all over the Grand Strand of Myrtle Beach. Whether you are looking for water slides or a lazy river, you will find one that suits your needs. There are also water parks that are just perfect for the family. If you are looking for a place to cool off, then pick a day of your vacation to spend at one of many water parks available. Splashes Oceanfront Water Park will allow you to splash your way into fun as you enjoy wet and wild water flumes, relaxing lazy river, kiddie pools, and speed slides. If you would like a different experience, check out South Carolina's largest water park called Myrtle Waves Water Park near Broadway at the Beach. There are twenty acres of waves and chutes run by more than a million gallons of water. The entry fee cover a full day of all the rides including their newest addition called Rockin Ray.

If you are looking for an adventure that includes mini golf and water slides then you should pick, Wild Water and Wheels. This park offer exciting rides and slides as well as eighteen holes of mini golf. My favorite since childhood are the bumper boats and go carts. There also rides for the youngest in the family. The whole family will find something they love about this Myrtle Beach water park.

49. Fill Up On Down Home Cooking

If you don't live in the south and you would like to enjoy some real southern cuisine then look no further than *Simply Southern Smokehouse*. If you are from the south, then you will swear your grandmother is in the kitchen! This stocked buffet is full of all the southern fixings. For the main course you can try each Barbecue, Fried Chicken, Barbecue Chicken, Chicken Bog, and Chicken and Dumplings. Their side items are to die for. Some of them are Sweet Potatoes, Corn, Green Beans, Rice/Gravy, Collards, Sweet Peas. You also can try a real southern style biscuits or go for the cornbread. If by chance you have room for dessert, you can have warm peach cobbler with vanilla ice cream like a grandmother made it. The banana pudding tastes much like my mom's recipe. I am only sharing just part of the menu options with you! If you only eat at one restaurant in Myrtle Beach, make it this one!

50. Take Care Of You

It is so easy to go on vacation and see many interesting things, go to wild attractions, explore amazing adventures but then leave feeling more exhausted than when you arrived. Yet we know the little saying that, "Nothing soothes the soul like a day by the ocean!" Vacation in Myrtle Beach is a great place to relax, breathe in the fresh ocean air, and make memories that will last a lifetime. While enjoying all that Myrtle Beach has to offer, also take time for yourself to reflect, look out over the ocean, talk to God, remember who you are, and soak up this beautiful place. Don't let the list of things to do and see be all that you experience on this special vacation in this little beach town. Take something deeper away from looking out at the vastness of the sea. You were made for more than just a thrill ride and a good meal. God, Himself, opens His hand and satisfies the desires of every living thing, and that includes you too. Enjoy, relax, soak up the sun, and remember who you are designed to be in this big world. Bon voyage!

Amy A. Sylvestre

Top Reasons to Book This Trip

- **Beaches**: You can stay all day and not get tired of taking in the amazing views of the vast Atlantic Ocean as you walk from pier to pier with sand in your toes and salt water in the air.

- **Food**: Seafood, steaks, burgers, low country cuisine, southern dining, and ice cream are all reasons to love Myrtle Beach!

- **Adventures galore await you here:** There are shows, fun rides, and experiences that you won't find anywhere else! Buckle up and have a blast!

Amy A. Sylvestre

> TOURIST

GREATER THAN A TOURIST

Visit GreaterThanATourist.com
http://GreaterThanATourist.com

Sign up for the Greater Than a Tourist Newsletter
http://eepurl.com/cxspyf

Follow us on Facebook:
https://www.facebook.com/GreaterThanATourist

Follow us on Pinterest:
http://pinterest.com/GreaterThanATourist

Follow us on Instagram:
http://Instagram.com/GreaterThanATourist

Amy A. Sylvestre

> TOURIST

GREATER THAN A TOURIST

Please leave your honest review of this book on Amazon and Goodreads. Thank you.

We appreciate your positive and negative feedback as we try to provide tourist guidance in their next trip from a local.

> TOURIST

GREATER THAN A TOURIST

Our Story

Traveling is a passion of the "Greater than a Tourist" series creator. Lisa studied abroad in college, and for their honeymoon Lisa and her husband toured Europe. During her travels to Malta, an older man tried to give her some advice based on his own experience living on the island since he was a young boy. She was not sure if she should talk to the stranger but was interested in his advice. When traveling to some places she was wary to talk to locals because she was afraid that they weren't being genuine. Through her travels, Lisa learned how much locals had to share with tourists. Lisa created the "Greater Than a Tourist" book series to help connect people with locals. A topic that locals are very passionate about sharing.

Amy A. Sylvestre

> TOURIST

GREATER THAN A TOURIST

Notes

Made in the USA
Columbia, SC
19 April 2021

36409359R00057